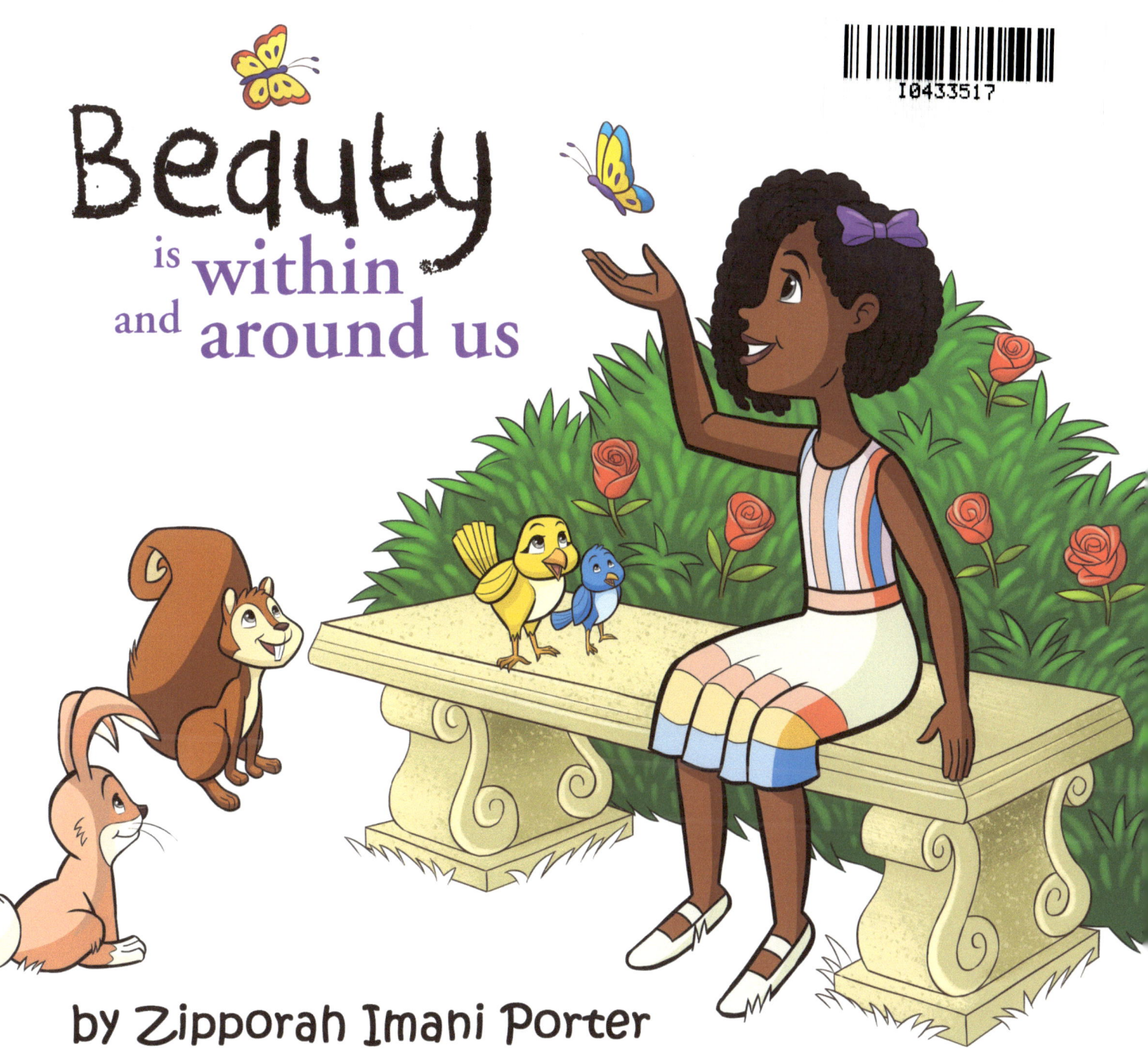

Beauty is within and around us

by Zipporah Imani Porter

Illustrated by Marvin Alonso

Beauty is within and around us

Copyright © 2021 by Zipporah Imani Porter

All rights reserved: No part of this book may be reproduced or transmitted in any form or by any means, electronic or mechanical, including photocopying, recording, or by any information storage and retrieval system, without permission in writing from the copyright owner.

ISBN 978-1-953585-00-4

Acknowledgments

My family inspired me to write this book: I thank my mom Estacy my dad Demarlo, my sister Nina and my 2 brothers Zion and Hez.

I want to thank my mom: She mostly inspired me because she is an author.

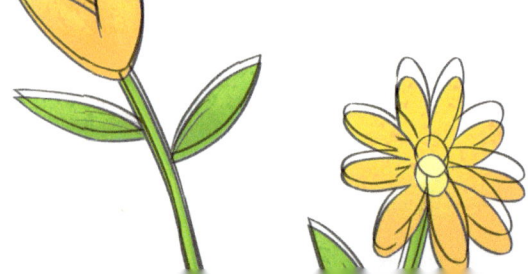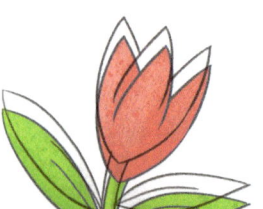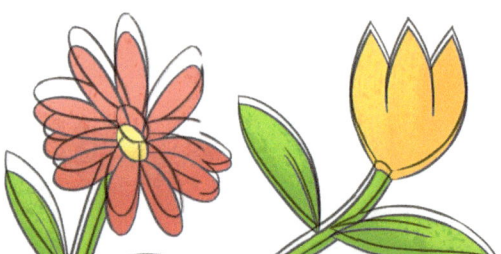

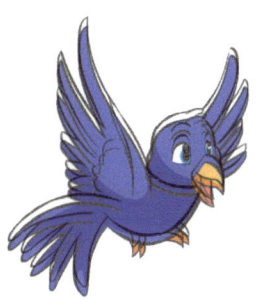
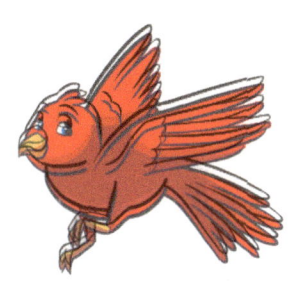

This book belongs to

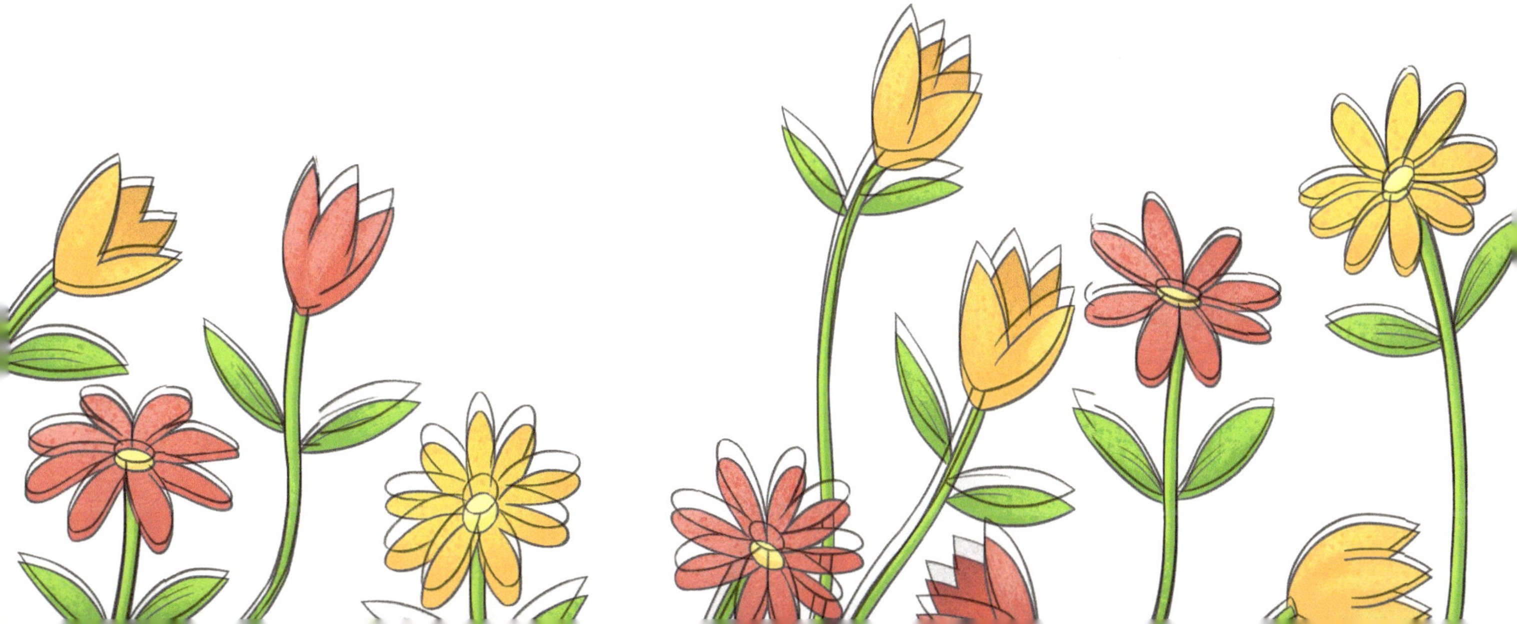

_____

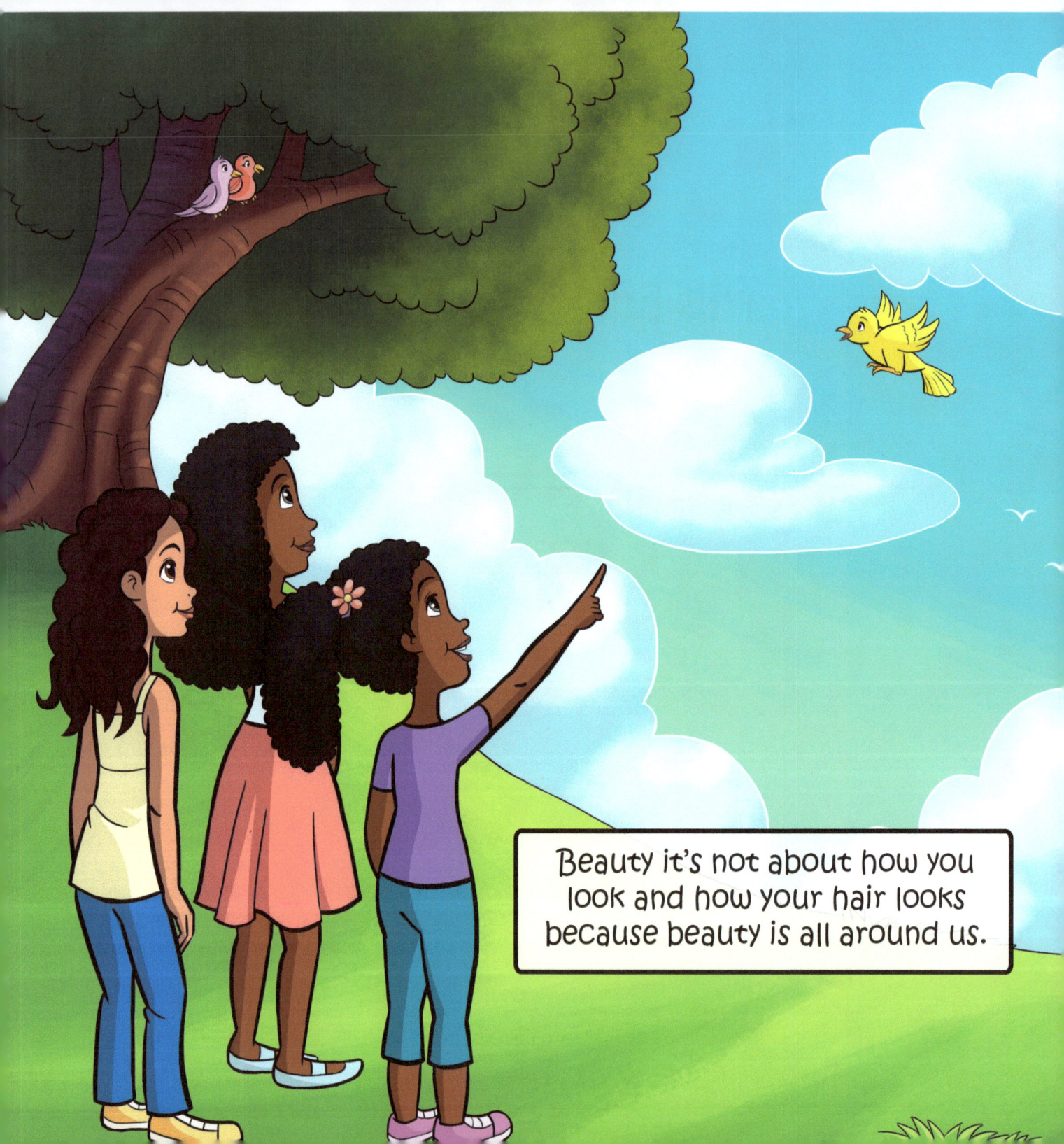

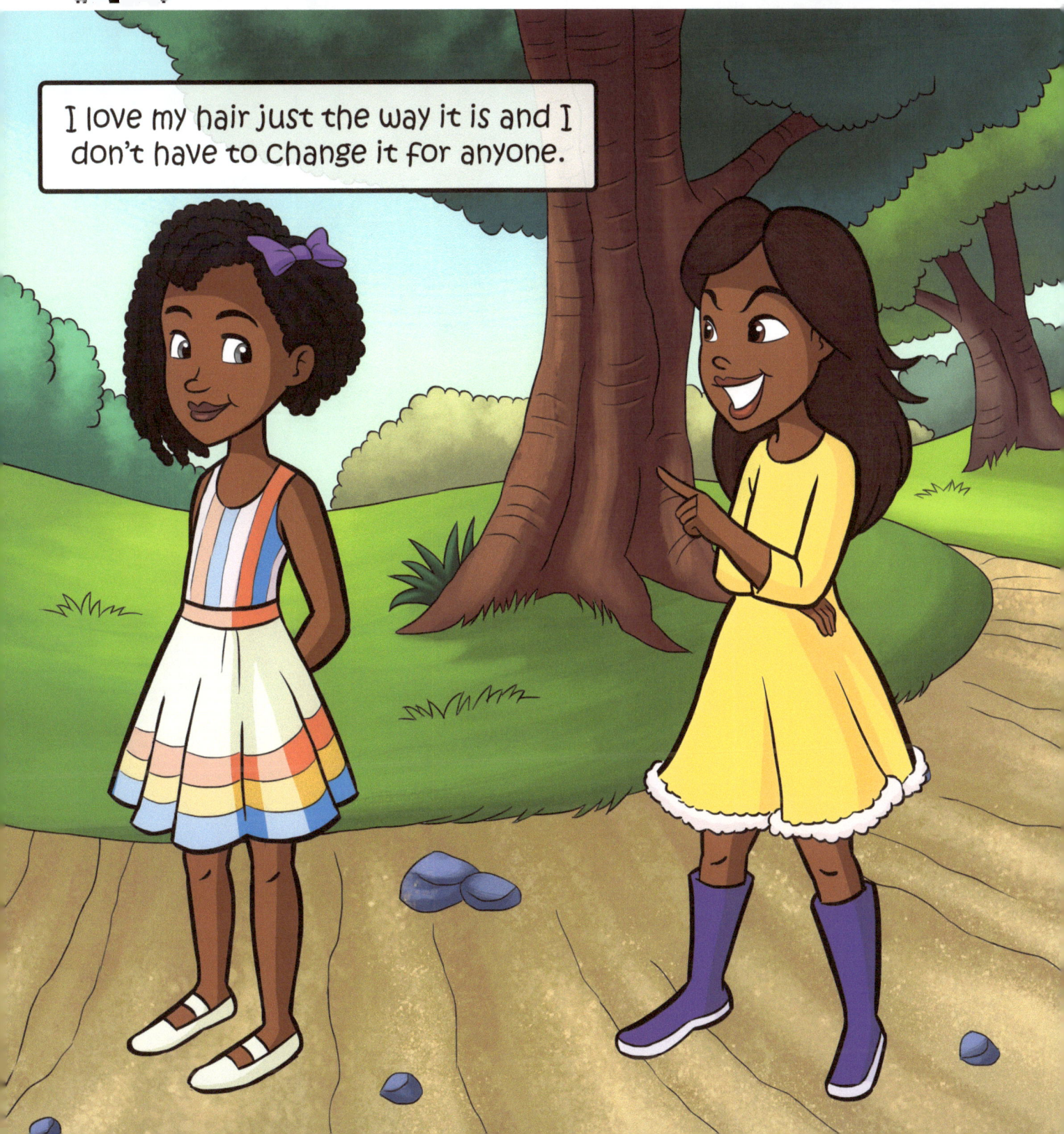

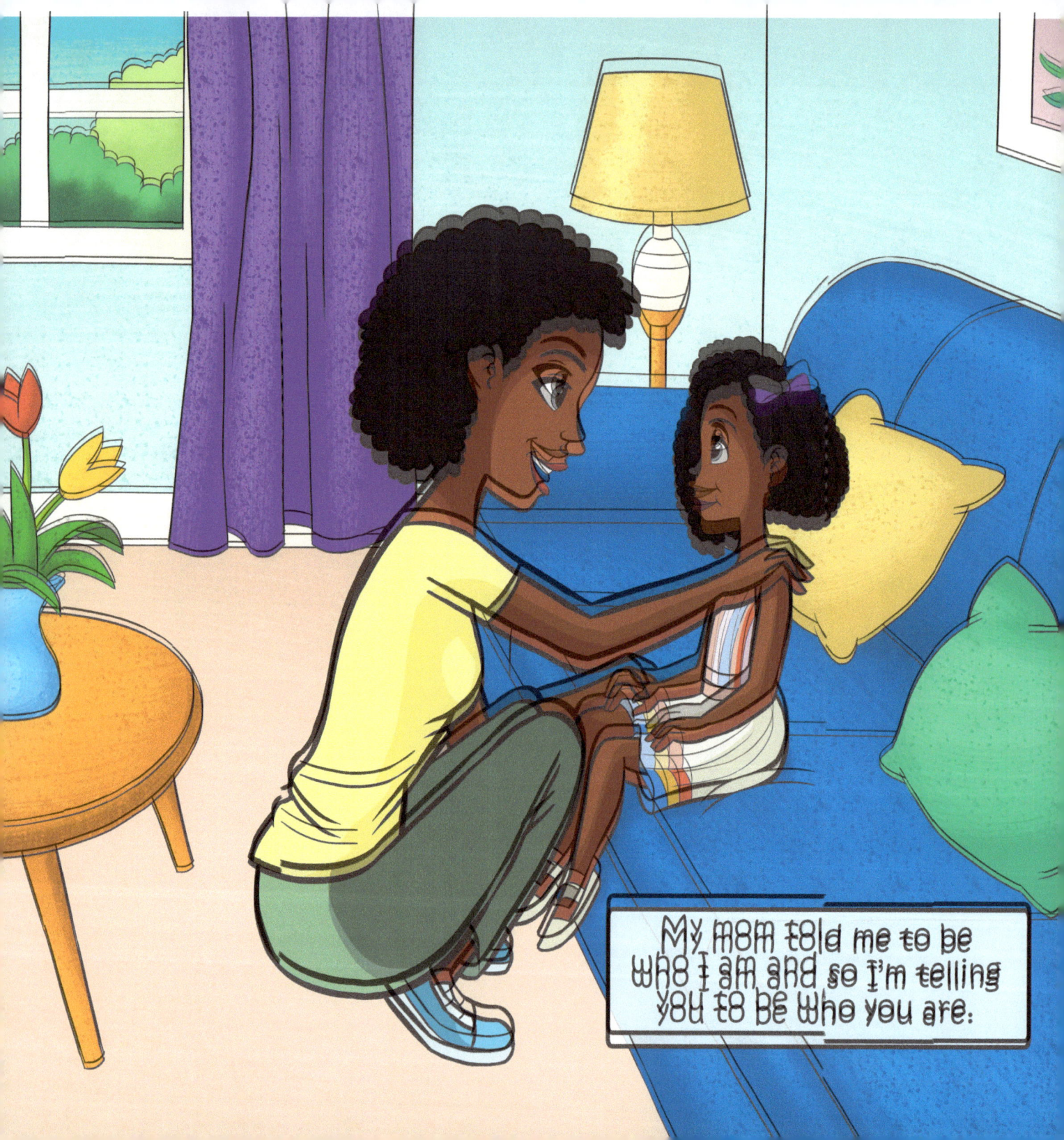

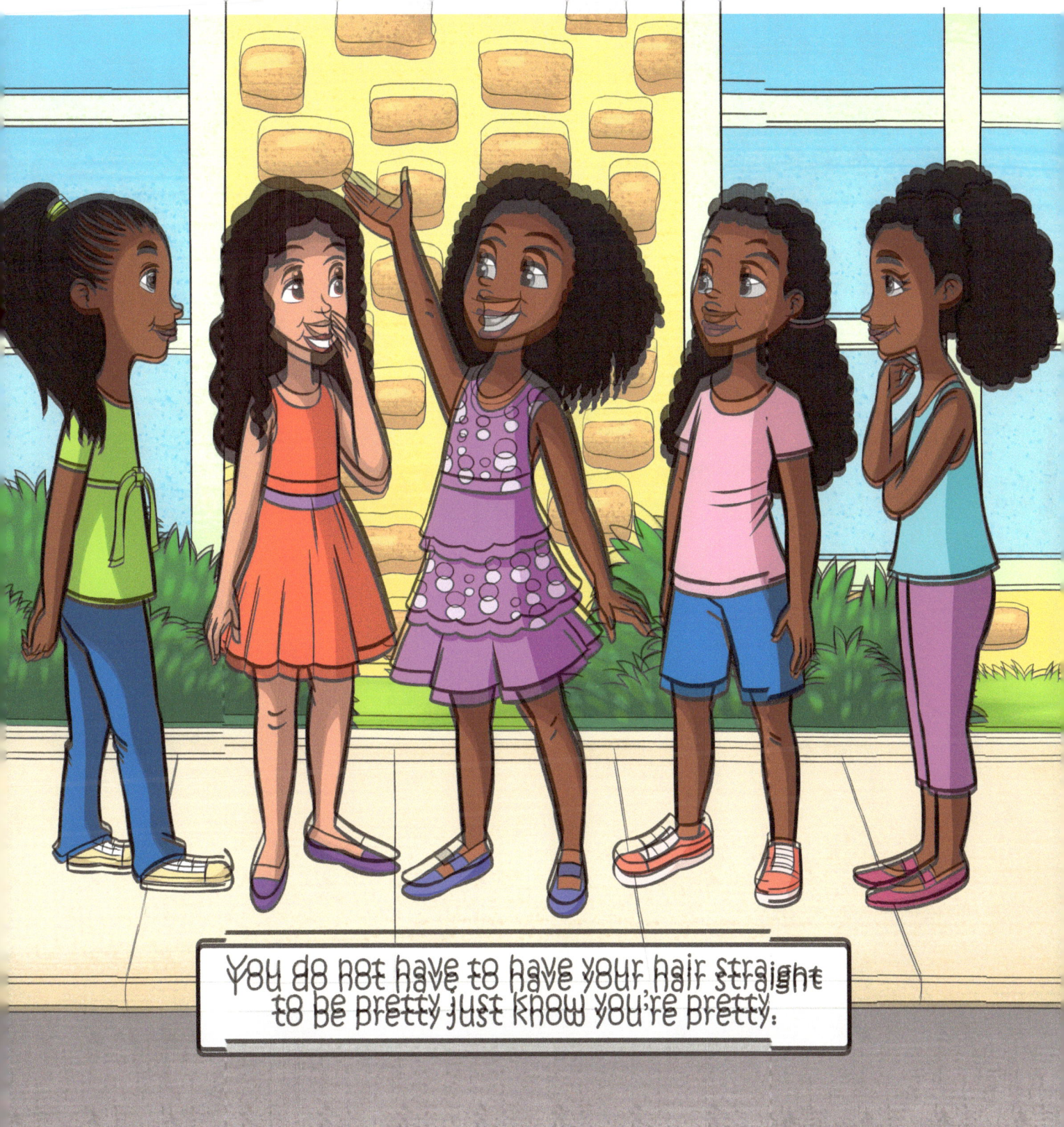

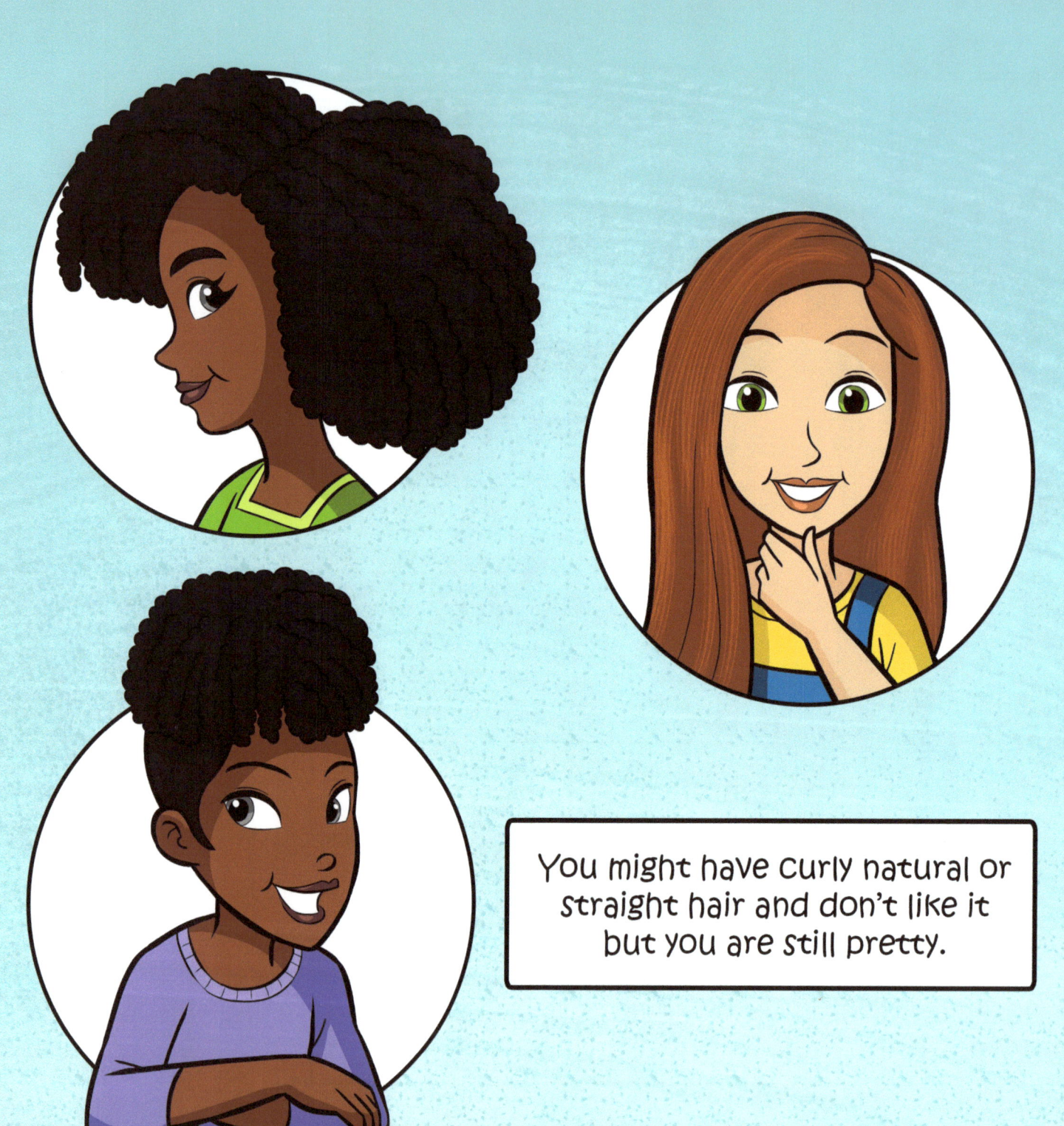

You might have curly natural or straight hair and don't like it but you are still pretty.

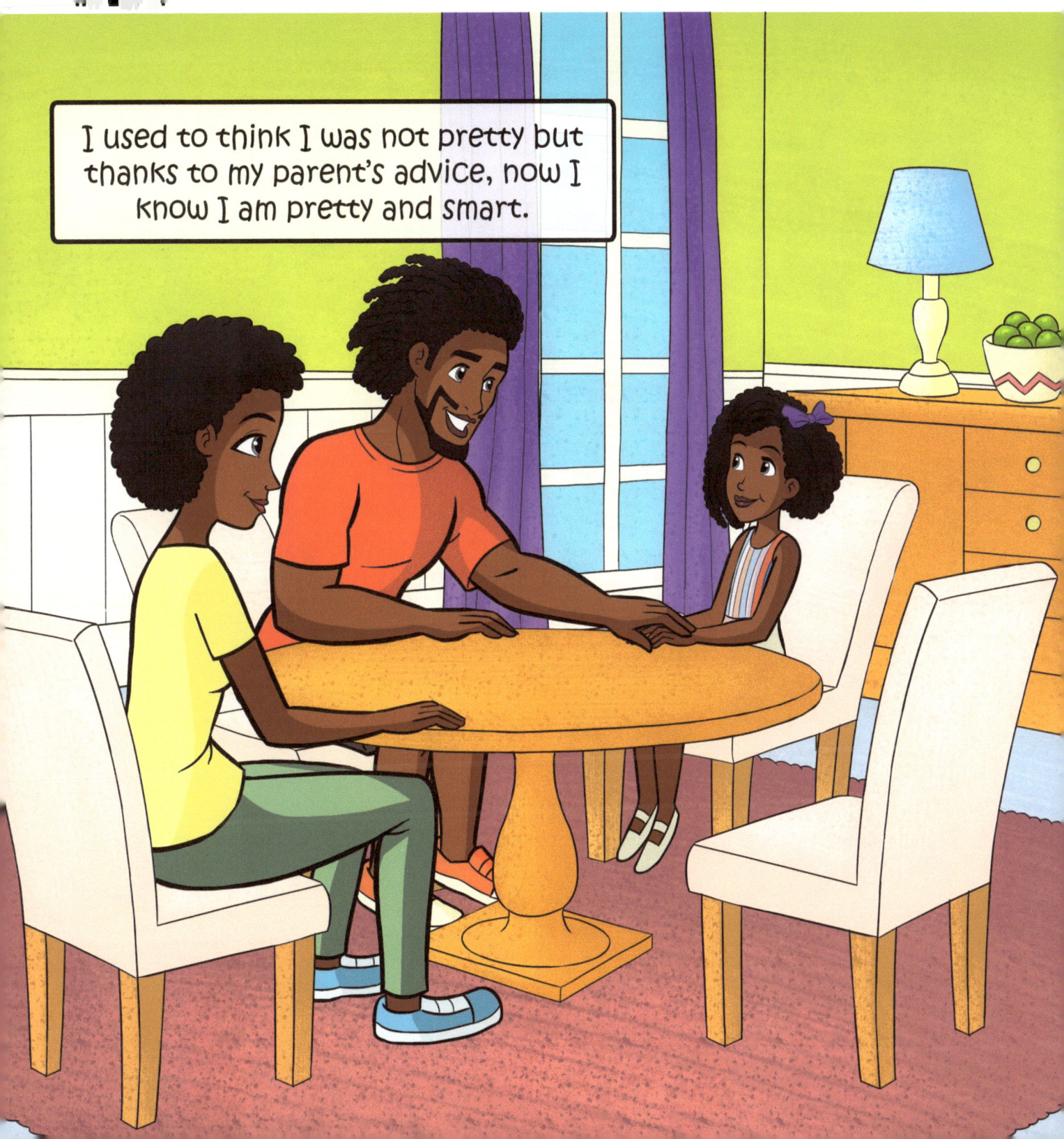

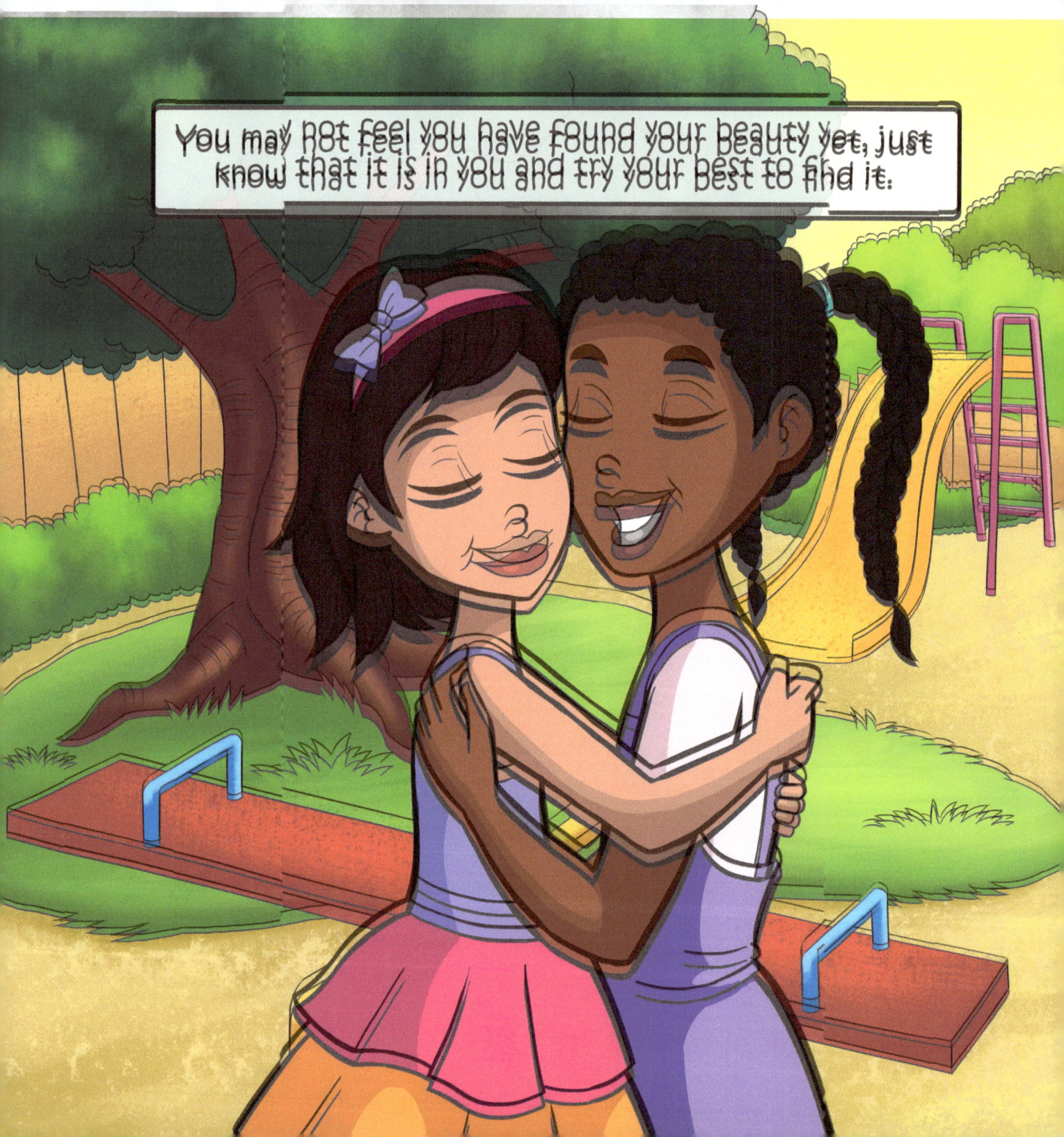

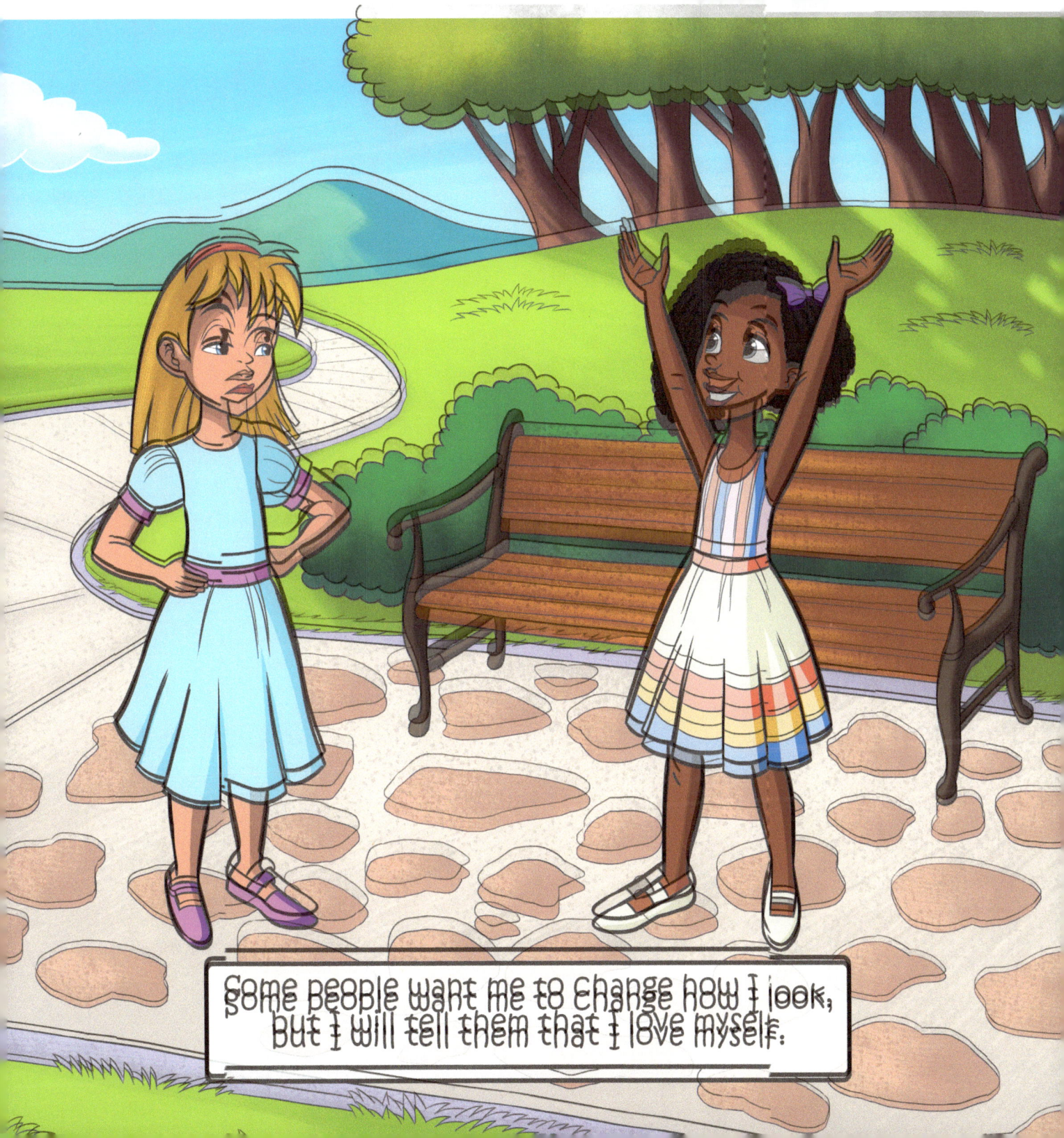

Some people want me to change how I look, but I will tell them that I love myself.

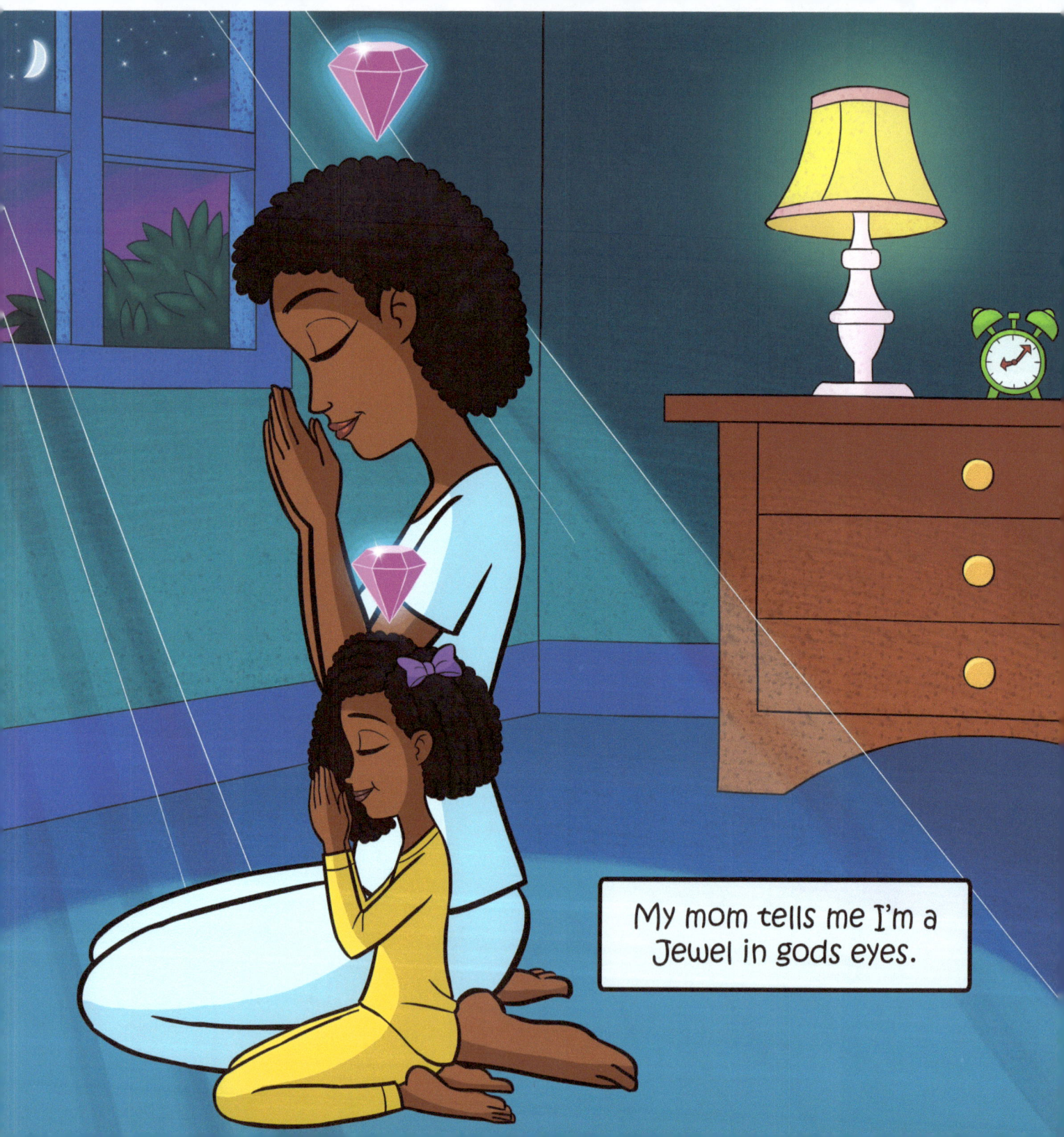

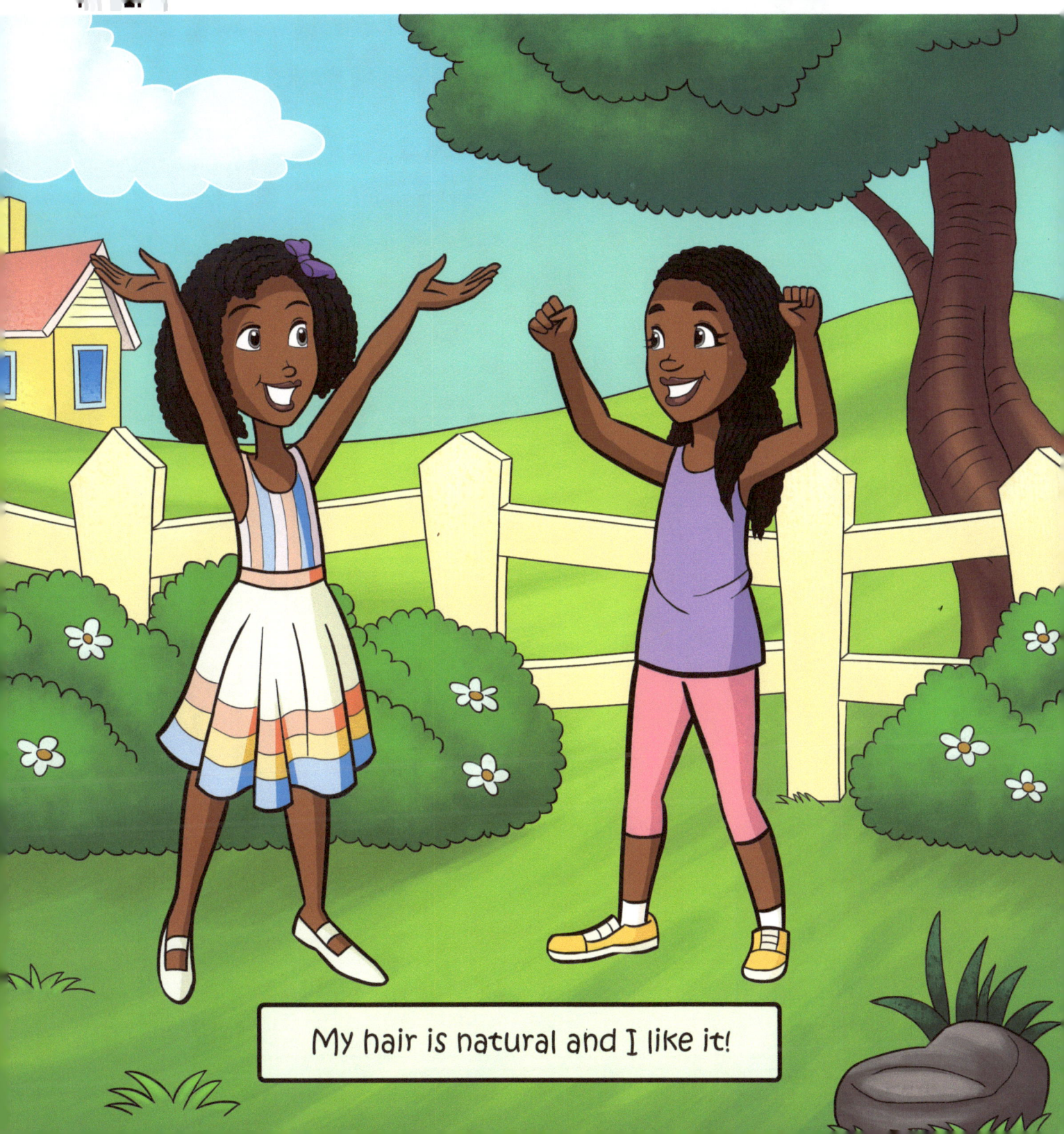

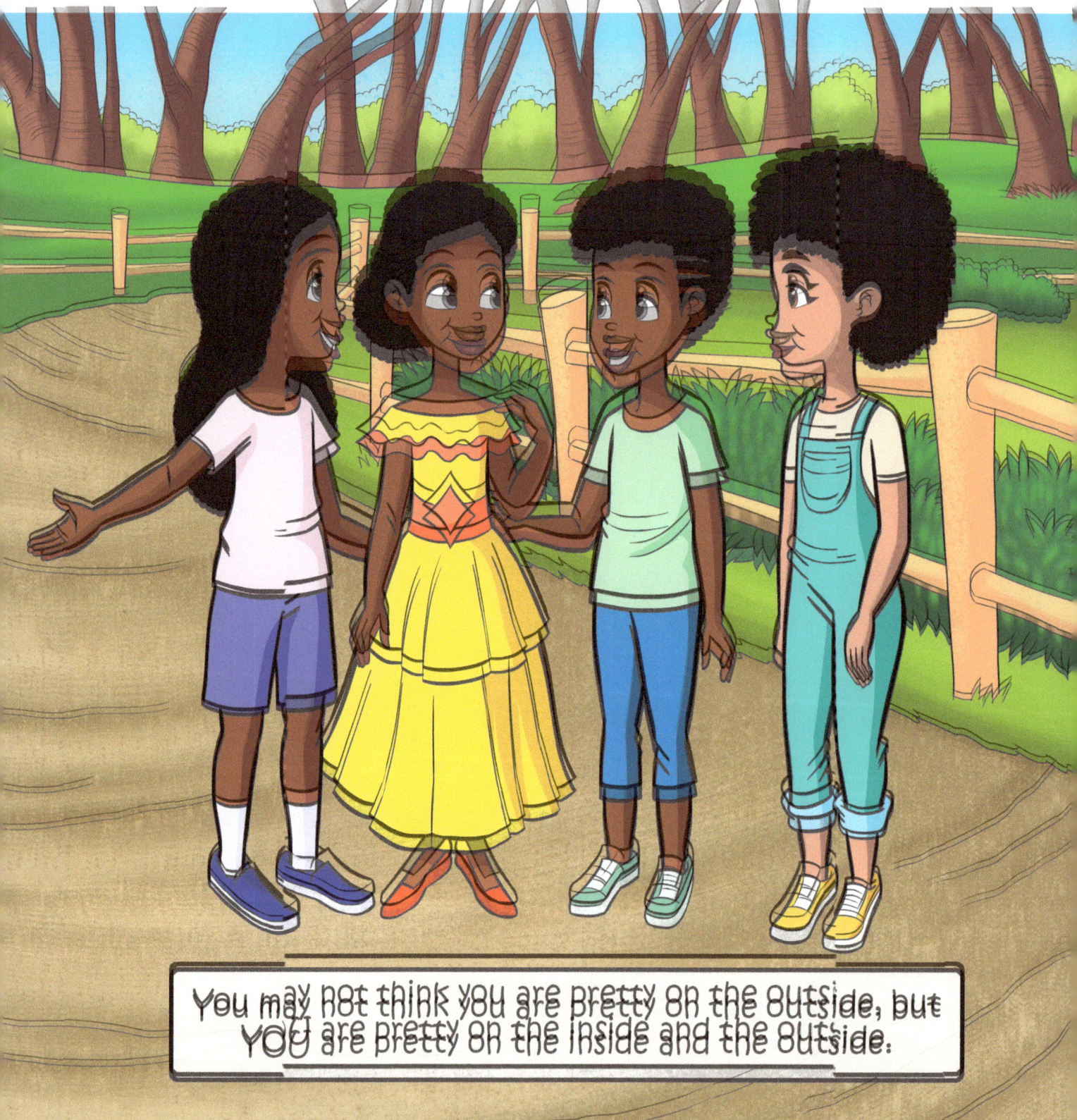

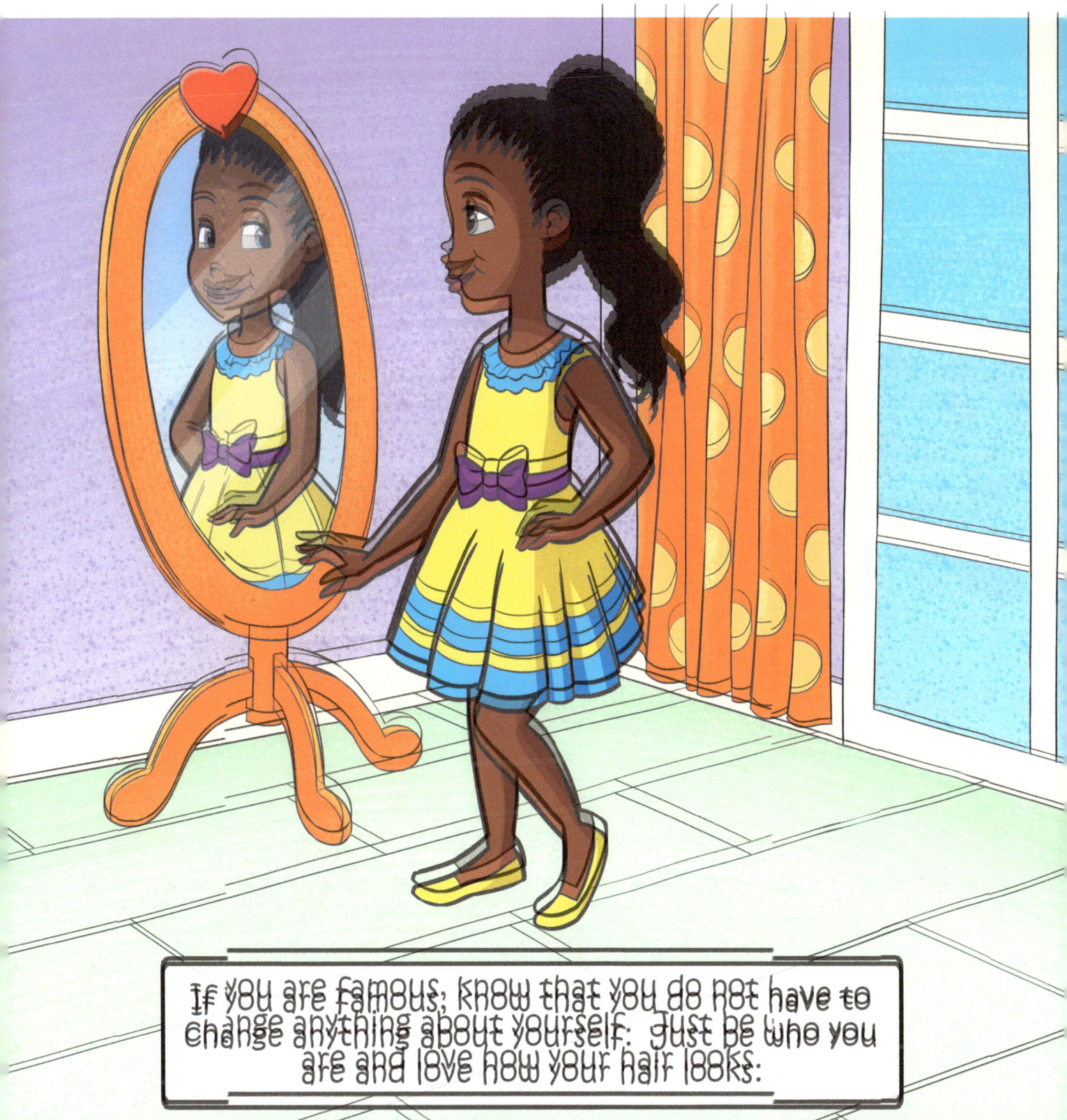

If you are famous, know that you do not have to change anything about yourself. Just be who you are and love how your hair looks.

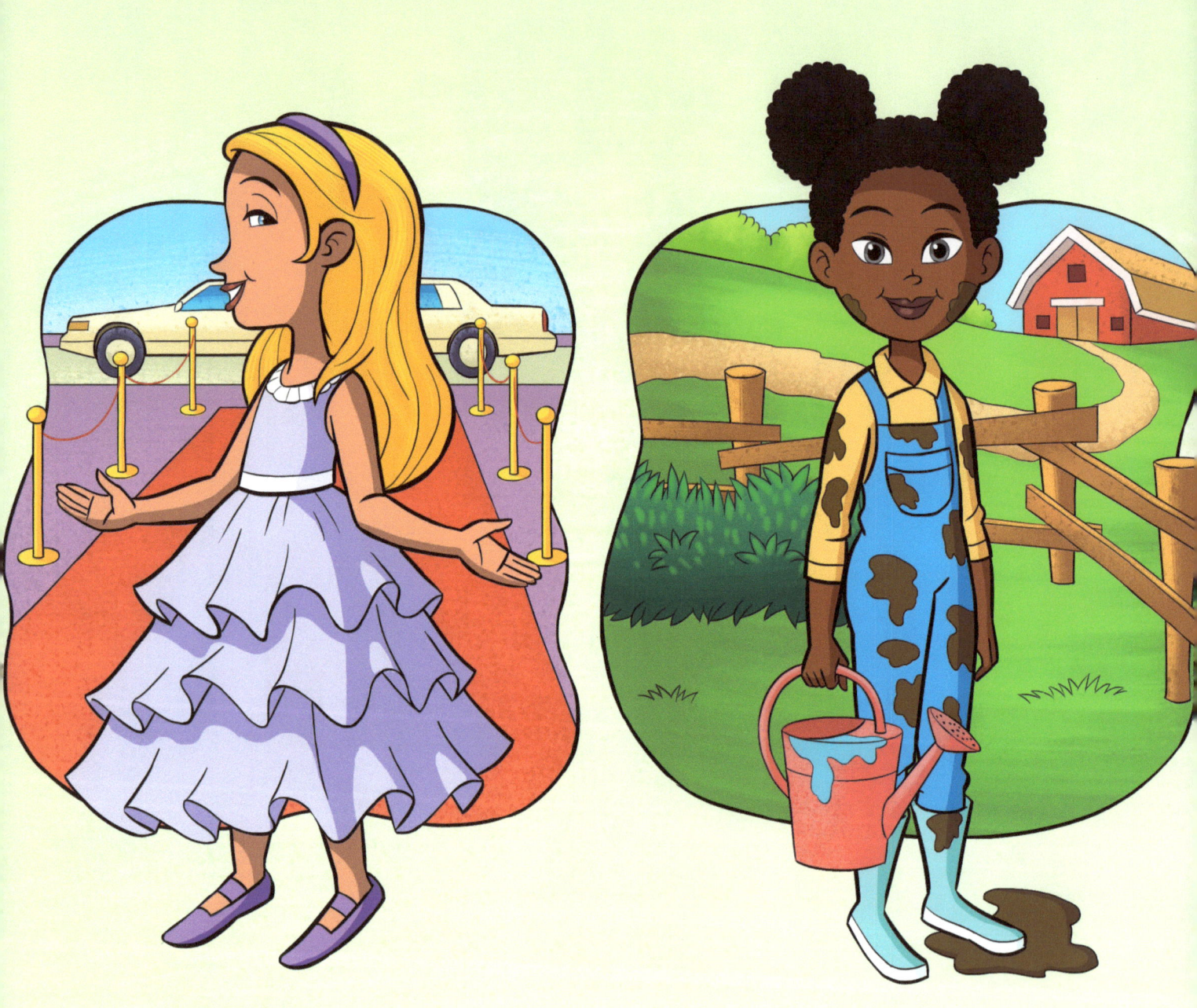

Beauty does not have to be wearing makeup or fancy clothes.

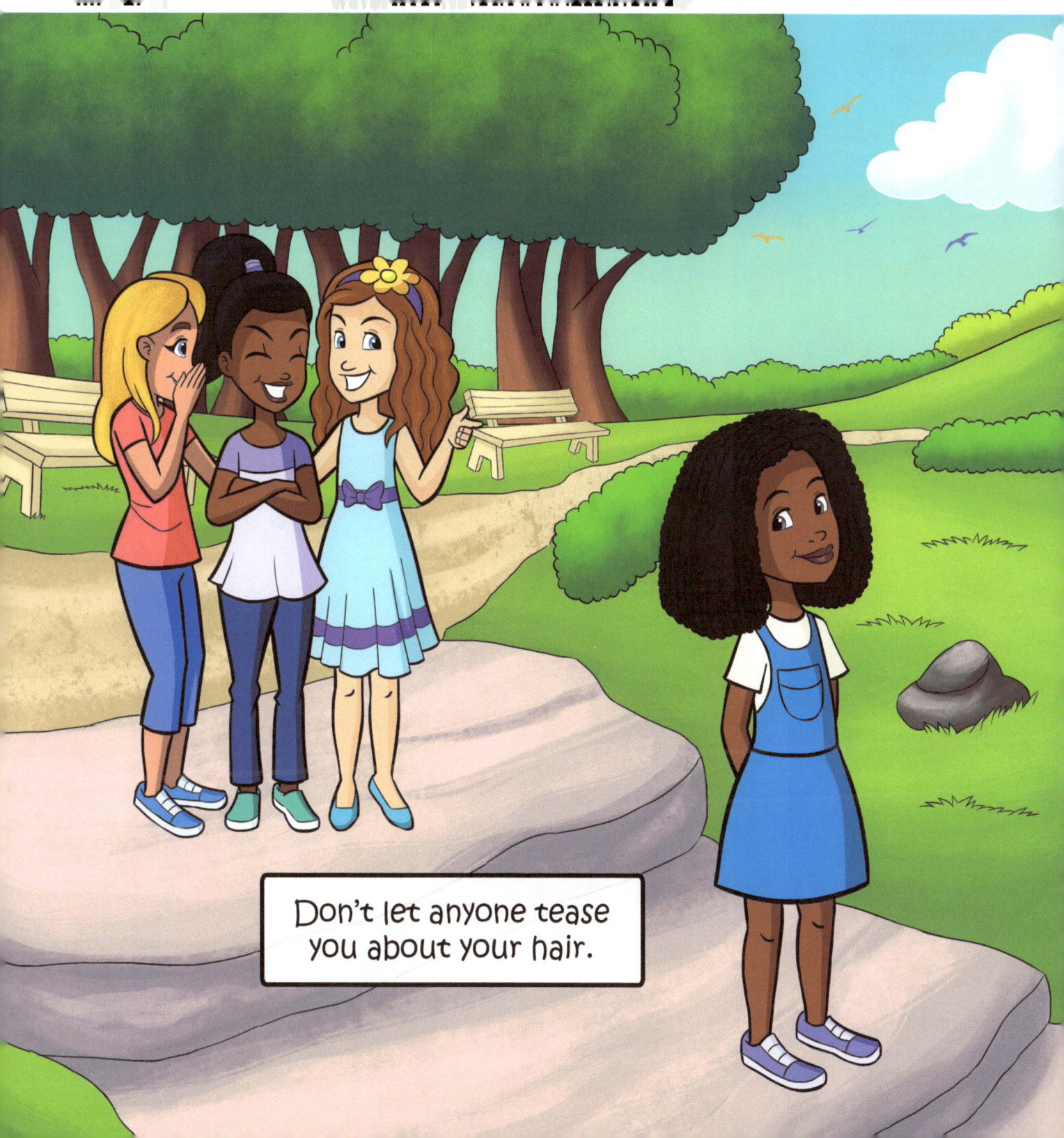

Don't let anyone tease you about your hair.

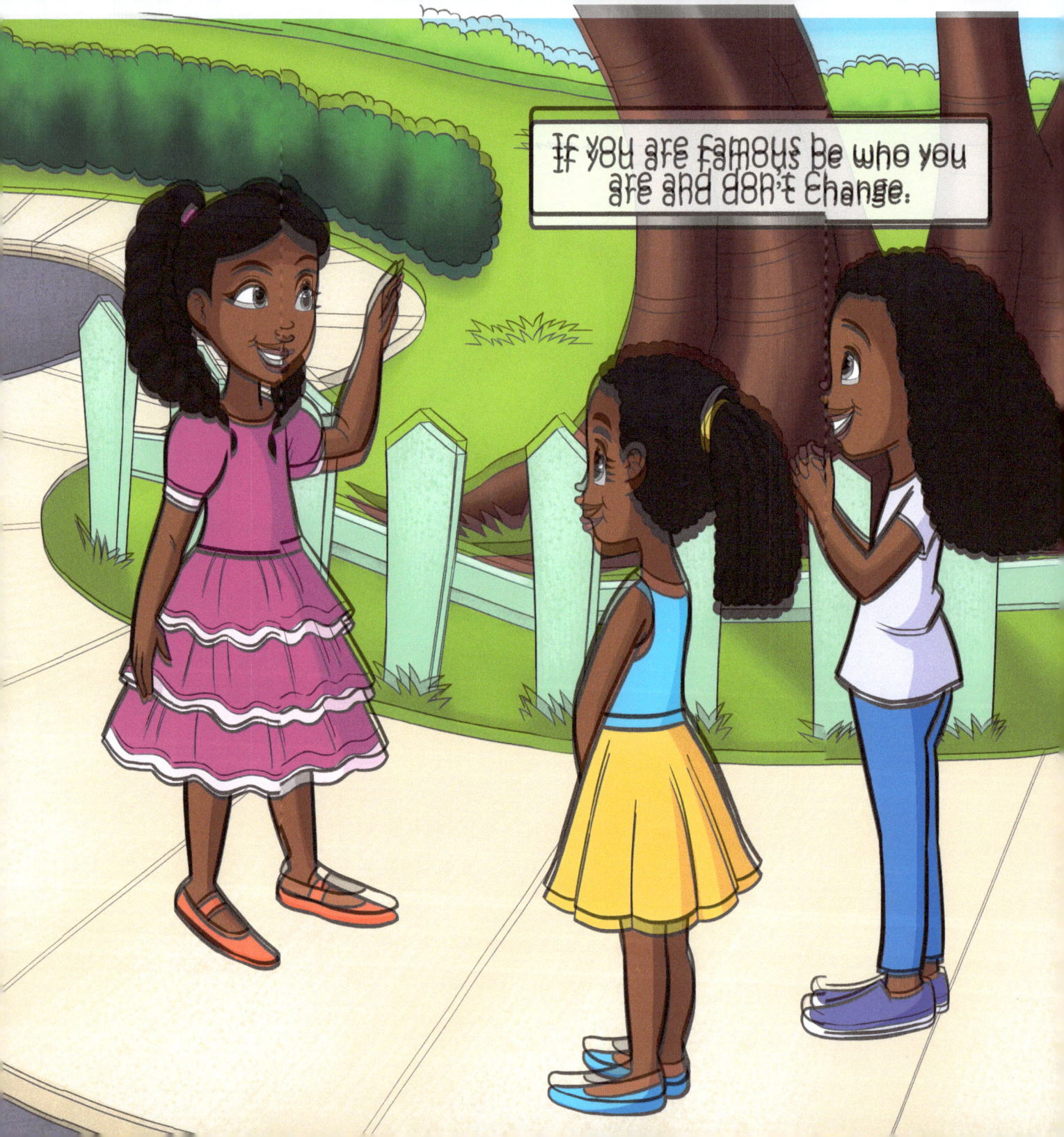

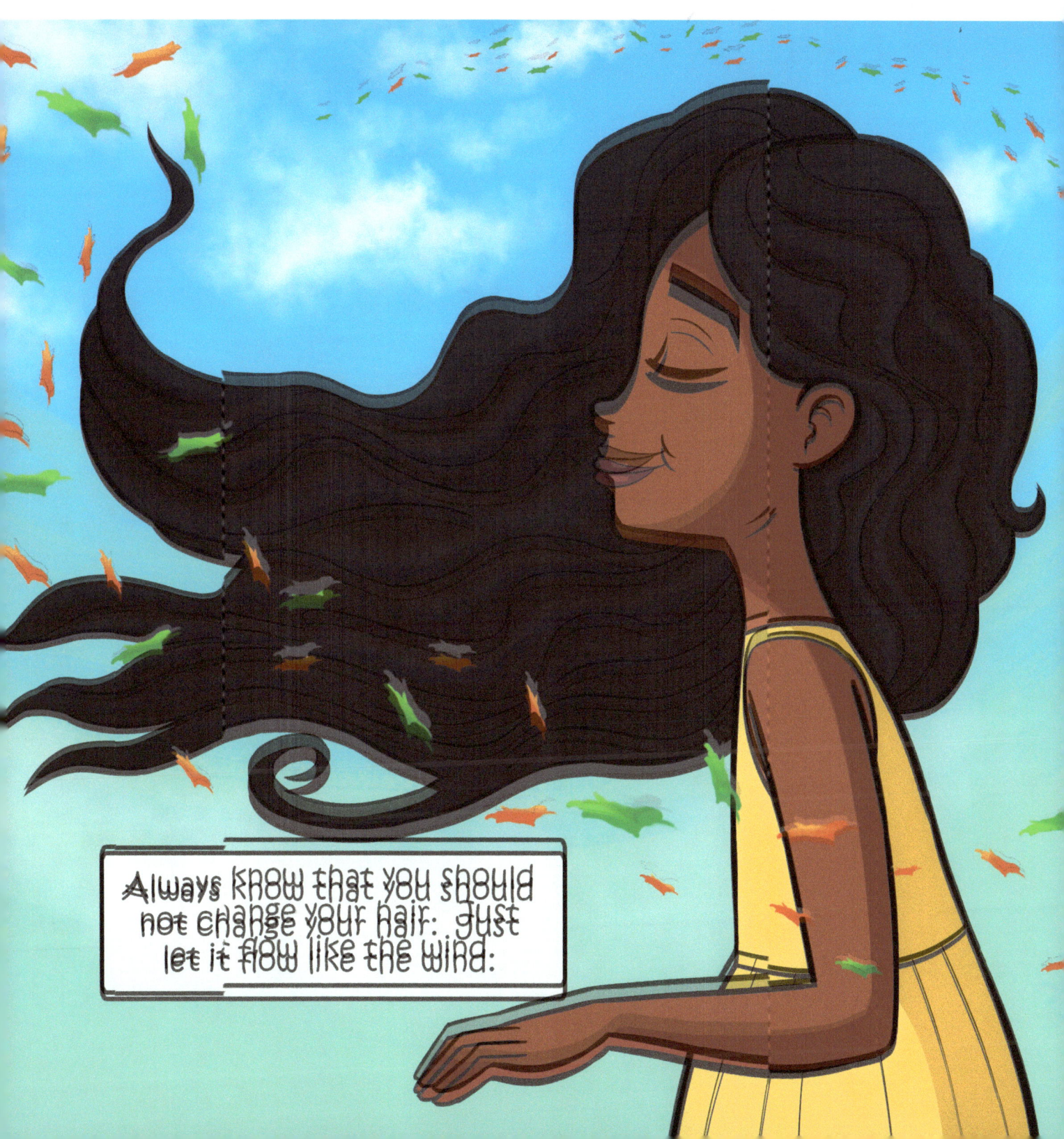

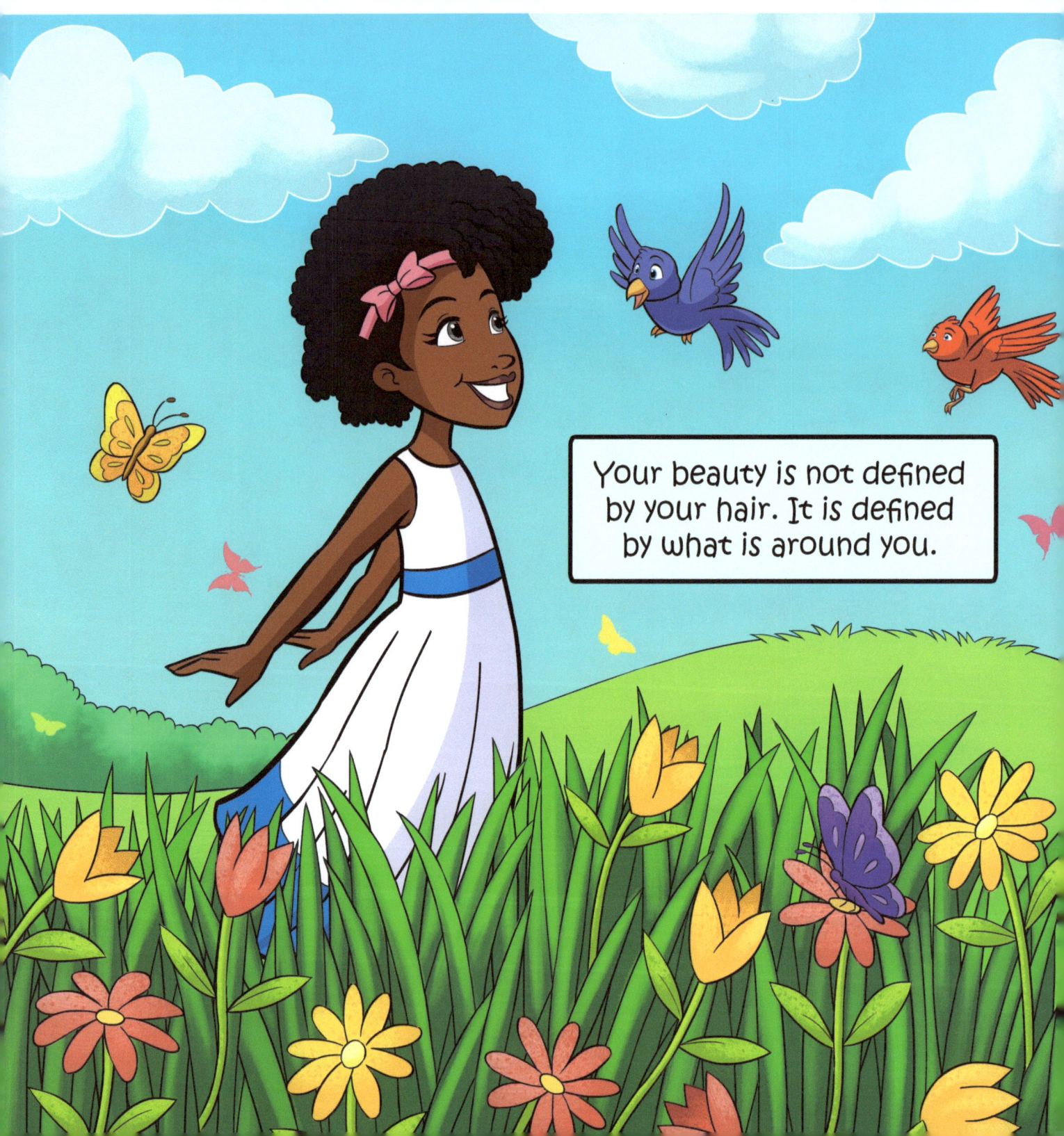

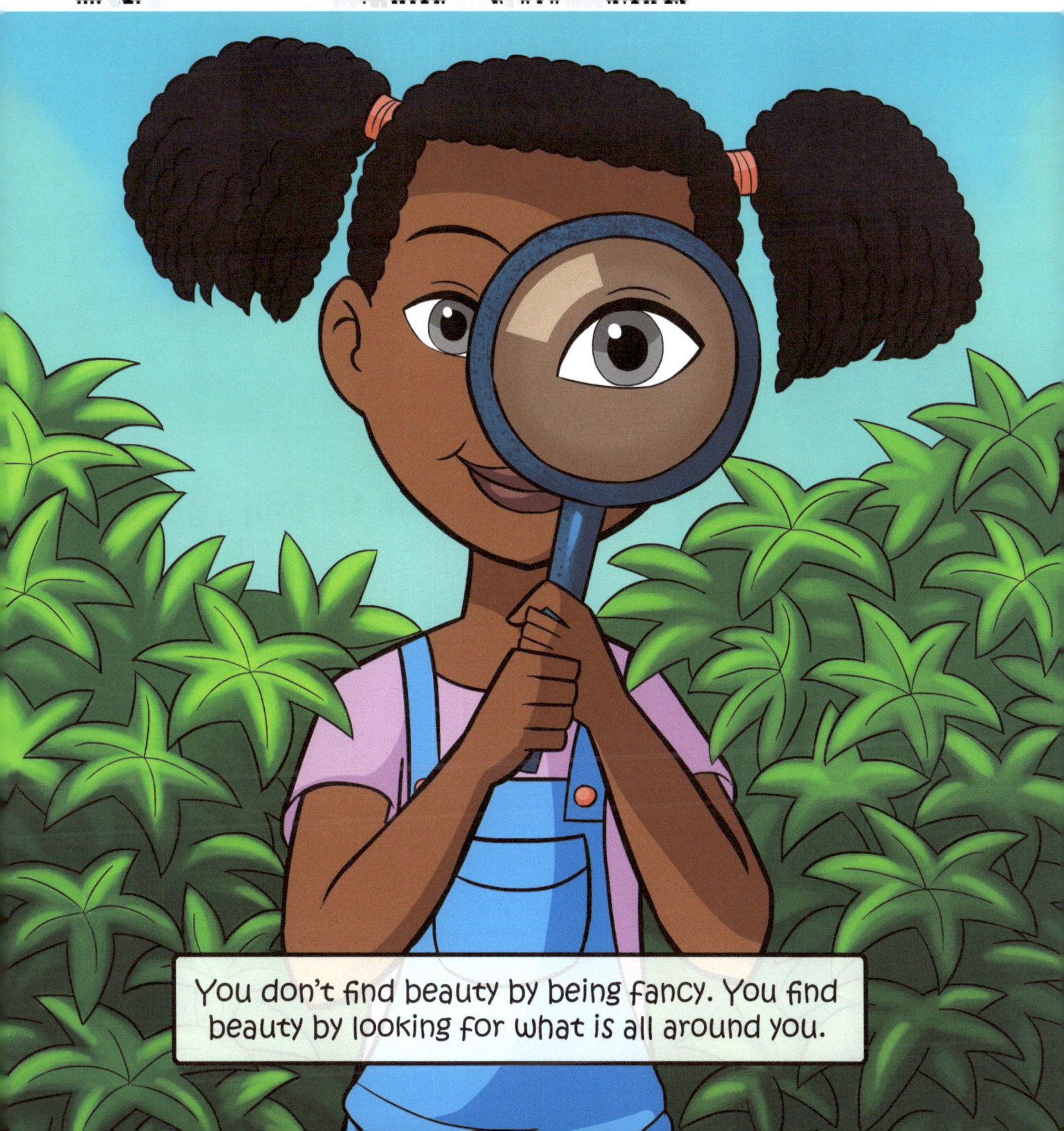

Zipporah's advice to you

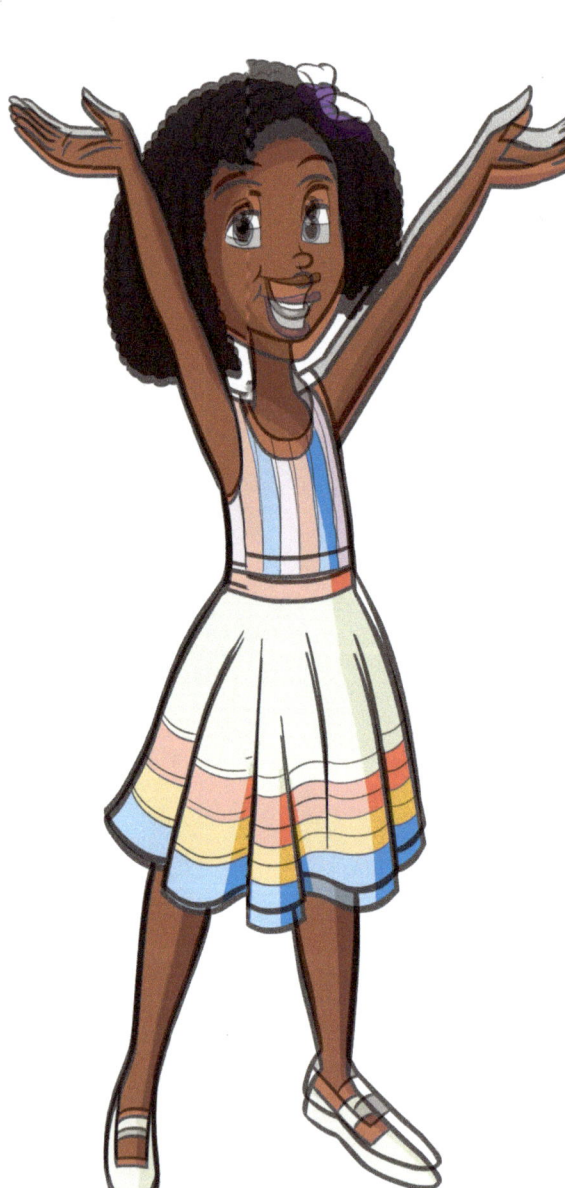

"I want to tell you to never give up and always keep trying". Do whatever your passion is and don't let anybody stop you".

I am beautiful because _____

www.ingramcontent.com/pod-product-compliance
Lightning Source LLC
Chambersburg PA
CBHW051944210526
45473CB00006B/2368